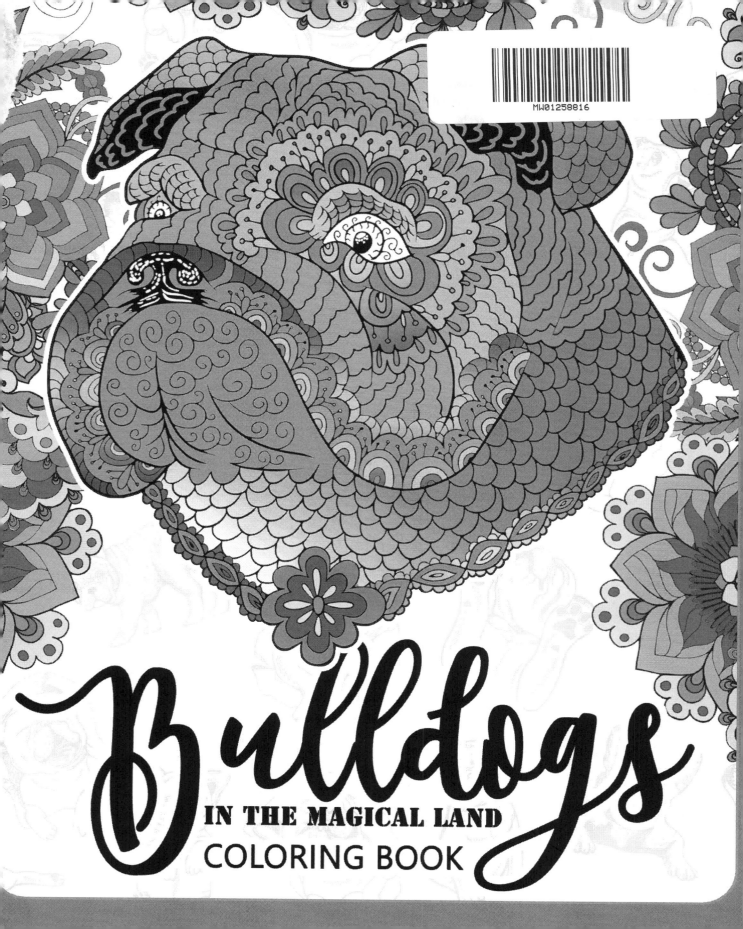

Bulldogs

IN THE MAGICAL LAND

COLORING BOOK

Because you know that

the testing of your f...

Bible Verse about F...

Dream Catcher Coloring Book   ISBN : 978-1546311560

NOTHING

WHILE

...MES

...ILY

ISBN : 978-1530381227

Free Download Coloring Pages

At : bit.ly/get_sample_free

V Art Studio

Exclusive Offer
ONLY V Art Studio Fan Club!!

Join V Art Group : *http://bit.ly/join_cover*

- Coloring Challenge : Selected Works will be published in Our New Release and you also will get the commission of Sales (First 3 Months)

- Participate in Creating Our New Book : Book Cover Vote , Coloring Idea and more.. / Your name will be appear in our book.

- GET Free Coloring Pages/ New Coloring Books for Our New Release.

- Much More ...

Join Us at : *http://bit.ly/join_cover*

 V Art Studio

Made in the USA
Middletown, DE
22 September 2023

39002350R00029